1995

Still Life In The Physical World

Gayle Kaune

Still Life In The Physical World

Blue Begonia Press • Yakima

CREDITS

Grateful acknowledgment is made to the editors of the following books and magazines where these poems first appeared:

Bellowing Ark for "As When A Fly Lands On Your Page," "This Water," and "These Wildflowers"
Caesura for "Labyrinths Were Designed As Pilgrimages"
Calapooya Collage for "Von Willebrand's Disease"
Crab Creek Review for "Monday Morning In October" and "Degrees Of Light In An Affluent City"
Embers for "Suddenly I'm Surrounded By Iris," "This wild field," and "Women's Retreat"
Everybody Bring A Dish by Shalom, United Church of Christ for "The Wren in Price Chopper"
Kalliope for "Symbiosis" and "Second Opinion"
Milkweed Editions for "Case Study" in *Looking For Home*
The Oregonian for "Remembering Yucca Flats, One Fall Sunday"
Poet and Critic for "Family Inheritance"
The Seattle Review for "The Poet Brings Her Mother To Her Reading," and "A Word By Which A Thing Is Known"
Willow Springs for "Returning To Richland"
Windless Orchard for "Amnesia"

Also: "Second Opinion" and "A Word By Which A Thing Is Known" won Washington Poets' Association awards in 1985 and 1988. "Remembering Yucca Flats" won a Ben Hur Lampman award, 1982. Several of these poems appeared in the chapbook CONCENTRIC CIRCLES, winner of the Flume Press award, 1989, published by Flume Press, Chico, CA, 1989.

My thanks to Casey Huff and Elizabeth Renfro of Flume Press, Jim Bodeen and Karen Bodeen of Blue Begonia Press. My gratitude to Dixie Partridge, June Baker, the Rattlesnake Mountain Writers, and William Stafford.

Cover painting by Ann Bowker.

Blue Begonia Press   225 S. 15th Ave   Yakima, WA 98902

For Bill, Lauren, Amy

TABLE OF CONTENTS

I.

II.

III.

IV.

V.

I.

And the white-haired jeweler from Denmark is carving
A perfectly faceted wife to wait
On him hand and foot, quiet as a diamond.

–Sylvia Plath

STUDYING THE CHARTS

Maybe the world is everything we don't see—
—Richard Jackson

So one day you can barely
read the *Big E.* Nothing
to do with age, eyes go bad
at fifteen or forty-five. The paper
says this has happened to the town's
favorite doctor—almost eighty,
the one whose office is run
by a flurry of nurses dispensing
allergy shots day in and day out
until one afternoon you decide
the doctor must have died years ago.

Why can't we figure it out?
How to run a life without being
there? How to go through the motions—
work, sleep, sex, a midnight game
of backgammon, meanwhile you're off
cruising the Inside Passage.

When I was six I took that ship
with my family and the new puppy
my father had won in a bar
in Burwash Landing. All day and night
that malamute down in the hold howled
till the whole ship went crazy.
We pretended he wasn't ours.

Father and Mother dressed for dinner
every night, sipped tall drinks
named "Tropic of Passion," collecting
tiny parasols until the black steward
who called me "Princess," cleared them away.
Everyone bet on a cardboard cut-out
horse-racing game, and one of my parents'
new friends squeezed through
a porthole and tried to drown.

Father and the other men pulled
her out—a strange underwater trophy
awarded for just being there.
As the Captain yelled the ship
back to port, the sad lady
kept talking on and on
about wanting to see Whitehorse. .

Later, when we drove there,
I kept looking for that horse.
I had a terrible cavity
and had to have a tooth pulled.
Afterwards, my parents bought
me a wolverine and leather jacket
from an Eskimo, the word *Yukon*
handsewn in a crooked, beaded line.
I liked that a lot; the name
of our dog! I had just learned to write
all my letters, was beginning
to read the signs.

AGE OF FAITH

In those days we were drunk
with moments–green lime islands
floating in the heat of summer.

Late afternoon, so still even
the birds hung on our words. Shaded
under California oak, sipping
gin and tonics with our friends,
we wove words through the scent
of eucalyptus, toasted dissertations,
with long, bare arms.
Our voices played like wind
chimes in the approaching dusk.

That night in a cathedral we listened:
echoes–Gregorian chants. The choir,
in sackcloth, carrying candles,
sang slow, repentant paces up the nave;
their plainsong sending us back
to that other faith, unshaken.

WINTER: *THE TAHOE QUEEN*

The Lake knows our secrets:
how we joined this dinner cruise
filled with honeymooners and
three white-gowned brides.

How just as Pauline and Joe,
our dinner partners, stack
cutlery and money schemes
into silver pyramids

we shuffle what is real.
Is it the iron lake and heavy
sky I felt standing on the bridge,
the boat plowing black water

into wide furrows as if waiting
for a body to be planted?
Or is it the pale bride in creamy
satin, crushed against the splintered

railing, holding her new groom's young
son, who's dressed in three-piece
suit, his pink carnation
sucked away by the wind?

Joe talks of the sponsorship plan,
invites us to a meeting
at the Holiday Inn when we return
to the City. And I am counting

dollars and dreams in my dinner
cruise head. Those young brides
married less than an hour;
ourselves, seventeen years.

Pauline and Joe, I don't know,
having just met when the waiter,

who wears his hair moussed
and serves our salad with a band-aid

dangling from his finger,
placed us together at this table
as I placed myself, earlier,
on the bridge hoping the wedding

photographer might catch me—cast
in gray, full-length coat—in the corner
of some picture: a solitary woman waiting
for this boat to navigate the distant islands.

LABYRINTHS WERE DESIGNED AS PILGRIMAGES

The woman loves the man.
This fact is not dreaded or imagined.
But it is as if a dream is what exists.
As if the repetitive nightmare of an Escher

tower, or stairs that lead both forward
and back keep them trapped
in a fairy tale of wrong doings.
Each action calls for the magic

of redemption or awakening but brings
only the glass dungeon of the dream
gone bad. The woman loves the man,
and knows his true smell,

but perhaps it is only the bedclothes
she has bleached in the wash.
Still, it belongs to them
just as their daughter's walk

and quiet hair belong to him,
just as her own handwriting has grown
into his and her gestures, both delicate
and mean, have expanded to include his puzzlement

that denies admission. The woman loves
the man but feels caught in this myth
that others might call good,
but she calls Cracked-Tile,

Water-Dripping-Like-Tears,
Endless-Trips-To-The-Well,
Back-Bent-Like-A-Crossbow.
She loves the man but longs

for the threads of a different story,
ones they tie together in a tapestry,
each color shimmering like a path,
a new way out.

THE DISTANT PROVINCES OF EMPIRE

One of us wears earrings purchased
from a shop named *Macchu Picchu*.
Small dolls draped in bright cloth
twirl and dance, as her head shakes
with the pain of telling her life
now, a woman finding her path.

I try to fashion my own truth,
but am carried by visions:
Macchu Picchu–how Nancy hiked
there with a friend, her marriage
going bad, saw hundreds of birds
rise from the ruins. She told us
later, "All those dead souls."

And how last year I lived
with my husband on Inca Parkway,
a street lined with Spanish houses
from the sixties. All summer
I watched blackbirds land
on the grassy median and thought
of those souls, and the ashes.

Now, in this dim room, six women
gather to discover the past.
The Incas had no written language,
the women turning to cloth,
weaving and reweaving each thread.

THE WOMAN WHO THOUGHT
MINNOWS WERE SPARROWS

—for Truus, a child's therapist

She dresses in taupe, gray, olive green;
is careful to stay in the background,
to help others find their own colors,
the ones from childhood palettes.

The woman who thought the word
"minnows" meant "sparrows"
really loses little in translation, she knows
it doesn't matter, they both mean
a shimmering mass (wings, fins!).

She hates small rooms
without windows, unless
they're filled with people;
loves the childlike art
of forgotten lands, the tortured

art of forgotten children—
a device, she thinks, like
herself, a mirror, someone to reflect
the past or future, a foreign
visitor who speaks only part

of the language, so others
can make their own interpretation,
pretend she's never startled
a school of minnows, or chased
a flock of sparrows to their wings.

THE WREN IN PRICE CHOPPER

–after a poem by Pattiann Rogers

There have been wrens trapped
in cathedrals, and how
they entered, a mystery.
But this wren flew
into the grocery store
through automatic doors and now
wax-white droppings spatter
the small-leafed mint and the broad-leafed
philodendrons, placed like a jungle
backdrop against the wall.

The wren flies from Picnic Supplies
to Videos. The storm outside
doesn't slow him down,
nor this fluorescent night.
He flits from throne
to throne, no pattern.
He is king.

And the woman, anxious, after seeing
him among the soup, and later,
crackers, finds a clerk in Produce
balancing melons on a stand.
"I know it's there, lady!"
the man snaps, as the wren
swerves to Shampoo,
"We've been trying to catch it for days."
The woman surveys the abundance of fruits
and vegetables; *Paradise*, she muses,
all those apples, and that bird, chirping.

And she knows they are no match
for the wren who wings quickly over
the iced case of one-eyed fish,
on his way to Wine, lands
on a display of iridescent
bubbles, and sings,

as if he were the last one
to fly aboard the Ark and all
the customers were drowning.

I I.

...salt margins
and stones that pulse...

–Margaret Gibson

AMNESIA

Suppose you lose your memory.
First, your personal history,
then things you know,
except for basics—Africa, Asia,
the square root of four.
But what you know, what I know:
poems, words, the line
on the page, years
of teaching history,
the intricacies of adoption—
all gone.

Sure, I'd be able to drive,
follow the day's routines.
Upon jumping into water
my arms would start to stroke,
feet kicking. But I'd forget
my name and all combinations
of words that I am.

Would I laugh at the same jokes?
And who are we without our
childhood—mine the family
that took three-month car trips,
Florida, Alaska, California;
not exactly normal. No word,
even now, for them.

And when I saw pictures
of my mother without
remembering our words,
would I sense our lives?
If I put my fingers
to the framed glass,
would they read her smile?

And every night, would I wander,
aimless, around my house after
tucking children to bed—

holding a pencil and an empty
notebook, wondering why?

Soon, I'd figure those two
girls I lived with were
my daughters, and the man,
their father, but nothing more.
We'd be what the mirror sees,
our bodies our only words.

THE WOMAN WHO WALKED INTO THE SEA

—for the man who saw her

You pace the beach,
suddenly waist deep in water;
eyes comb the blackness.
Nighttime, did the moon illuminate
her dress? Was this a woman who lived
near...which shore?

It's not that you'd been drinking,
only walking the sand with memory.
So even though rescue
workers could find no trace,
not even a pair of silver flats,
her iridescent purse;

And though they said it was the moon,
how its white-edged lines skirt the foam
causing men in their longing to see
the dark-haired daughter of Neptune,
her slip-like dress a shimmer
like salmon or barracuda;

And though they've taken you,
now, to this room with spotless
linoleum and are flashing your eyes
with flecks of light, you will not pretend
to forget. Even if they lock
you up again and give you the medicine,
this is the real story:
somewhere there is always
a woman for you, waiting,
willing to drown.

LOST LAKE

Hood River County, Oregon

At dawn I watch slow boats
row the deep shadows. Remember?
Twelve sisters pretend to sleep
then spend their nights dancing
in a distant palace, ferried
across the water in twelve boats,
by twelve princes.

For five days we camp with friends
along the shore. Our daughters
play Space War assigning giant stumps
the names of spinning planets.
The women prepare simple meals.
The men fish.

Nights, as the fire whispers,
we settle in our tent,
my husband's sleep so deep
he does not stir. Wrapped in down,
I dance in far pavilions,
return at dawn, *farewell.*

VON WILLEBRAND'S DISEASE

What I want to say about blood
is not acceptable. Women
must not discuss the warm clots
that slip between their thighs,
the fear that sometimes
this won't stop and soon your life
will drain away. What I want
to say about blood has to do
with men, their rapes
and knives, the awkward uniform
of war, how even our best
dreams can be slit to reveal
the work of shrapnel—no red
ooze able to glue
faces back together.

What I want to say about blood
has most to do with inheritance,
those genetic twists that leave
your blood unable to clot in the right
place at the right time, and thinly
persistent it continues to flow,
sometimes all night in your sleep.
You wake to find the pillow soaked
from only a cut; and your small
daughters become the frail vessels
you must guard, their seeping
scars badges of disease,
their pooling fear
a constant bruise.

SYMBIOSIS

notes from a mother to a daughter with anorexia

—nights of waking, wandering
through the nightmare forest to your bed,
my last, crying, daughter.
The moon sliced the darkness
with knives. Spiders
crawled their white webs
up vines and lichen. Leaves
hissed at us *shelter, shelter,*
so quickly were you quieted,
how was I to know the others
had sucked the sap dry?

Having no knowledge of weed
and flower, I fed you roots.
Nurtured on bark, some bitter,
you grew. The others sent
feelers, held fast against
demons; your tendrils curled
within. Now I wake, creep
into black to touch you,
my last, silent as moss.

–for A. F.

CASE STUDY:

Abuse, but the girl's
room clean, adequate. Father
and stepmother say they care
but have no space, except
the basement. Mother will take child
but only if custody reassigned
first, a matter of months...

The child regresses
from seven to a diapered three,
too timid to speak in school, in court,
too frightened to ask for a room
upstairs, away from spiders who live
in the basement, cool and dark—
an adequate home for arachnids
and little girls.

There, common house spiders, comb-
footed spiders, dance
all night on her pillow, drop
from the ceiling onto soft
eyelids, whisper secrets to her inner
ear. She wakes to these tangled
web-weavers hanging from drag lines,
their segmented bodies lit
by the moon caught in the window well.
And the girl cowers under quilts,
her eyes tracking the slight shadows
as they circle the walls of her room.

The spiders want only to be close,
their eight shiny legs always scurrying
near. All night while she jerks
in her dreams, their silk nets
connect bed to wall, drape
the rungs of her chair, vibrate
with their eager feet.

July 21st

–for A., after a transfusion

I want to find the stone
fish that swims the red
ocean, discover the onyx
clock that stops the white

hour of fear, take the best
memories of food and shelter,
dip them in gold leaf.

I want to take this day
and plate it with silver,
cast it in bronze forever,
then throw it away.

I want it solid and clean,
not this soil of blood
and hospital veins;

clean as light
lasered through skin,
sharper than metal
machined into needles,
pure as the slicing moon.

TURNING FORTY

You wake one day and you're there,
but it's nine months later until you
recognize the strange geography of your face,
follow brown hairs to grey roots, begin
to question butter, the caffeine
in tea. You lie beside your husband
and think of lovers, those past,
those never to be because you believe
in loyalty, want to believe in honor,
yet what will you remember
when you're ninety and in the Home
fingering the puffy cotton blankets
that shed lint like dog hair?

Your birthday: the children bought signs,
Look Who's Forty, made up a menu for the Ruby
Restaurant (did they know it was July's,
your bloody birthstone?), blew black
balloons with eager breath while your mother,
weak in her wheelchair, laughed, loving
all of you together. Later, the neighbors
came for a drink, his birthday also, only eighty.
And you were all so happy
visiting family, talking, eating,
choosing anything you wanted
from the Ruby Restaurant:
beer, tropical punch, wine,
and water at no cost.

SUDDENLY, I'M SURROUNDED BY IRIS

those strange flowers of childhood
that grew in old ladies' yards
—awkward with their phallic
tongues lolling, their petals
flopping like spaniel ears.

Suddenly, I'm collecting paintings
of iris: White Iris with San
Francisco Skyline–(the Bay
a brighter background
than any small-town lawn);

Watercolor
of Iris in Translucent
Vase (placed with a pencil
and children's crayons
on a cubist table).

Daily, I'm accumulating
iris, planting tubers–
White Excelsior, Purple
Sensation, Angel Wings–
and in my bedroom silk

iris take an erect
stance in Baccarat
vase (the thick glass
prisms their
accomplishment).

Mornings, I eat alongside Dutch
iris, blue with yellow tongues–
delivered by the florist,
stuck in the hidden sponge
of a broad arrangement of pink

gladiolas, whitened stock,
and yellow mums–rising
in a forest of maidenhair
ferns and sweet baby's breath.

AT THE CAROUSEL

It's hot for November,
dry air and the sun flying
a scarf of bright silk;
as if a merry-go-round

has reversed into summer.
And slowly gathering leaves
in this Fall haze, I remember
the blind man, mid-twenties,

at the carousel one August day,
years ago. How handsome he was, sitting
there, enchanted by the music.
And knowing my voice was lovelier

than my teeth, knowing my perfume
settled in the air in the same way
it might if I were beautiful,
I moved close and asked

if he wanted me
to describe what I saw.
Myself, sixteen, trying to carry
in words of color that which only

music can hold. *The children
are sturdy, their horses rise
bravely, the colors pounding
in a rhythm of grace.*

*Green wavers like the sweet
breath of fear; white is waking
to winter silence.
Blue might be water*

*if it's from the river,
or the cool heat of stars.
Red is the sun
when you move this way.*

And gently, I touched his face,
turning his eyes towards the light.
This gesture my first;
now I knew there would be other

faces, other afternoons.
The children are proud
as they climb off the horses
patting the sweaty manes!

I wanted to stay in the sun
forever, trying to find words
for that other thing:
to tell him the carousel

is like time—a circle
that travels forward or back,
or stalls, years later,
as on this autumn day

when I am lost
in that summer's heat; in love
with the music, my young self,
all the wild-eyed ponies.

STILL LIFE WITH MUTED COLORS

---for Maggie, Shelby

Is it enough to scatter blossoms
across bare dressers, to wear
clothes the color of apricots
and let our hair grow long,
even though we line our years
with wrinkled dreams?

A woman walks the beach
at Thanksgiving. She is with her lover
who will call three days later
and say goodbye.

We can always discuss this:
how driving the car one day
your passenger might jump out;
or a husband of twenty years leaves
late one afternoon when the light
is shifting. You have to read
his journal to learn he's really gone.

Everything fades to become part
of time, a linear desire we use
to order pain. There is no past;
it's here, now, in the brain's
chemistry and the way our breasts
memorized his body
that weekend at the beach.

We can have it all, and lose
it in the same breath.
We give ourselves roses
the color of peaches.
We smell their fragrance,
breathe their decay.

SECOND OPINION

She is an hour early for the doctor;
her husband drives through the pale
city to find a park. The children, caged
in the car since morning, have wilted like flowers;
their last hundred miles behind glass
spent sighing with a passion.

They find a park, their passion
for space indulged by wide lawns, the doctor
forgotten. In the garden she sees a glass
house, urges her family to enter its pale
light, wander among flowers;
fuchsias spilling from baskets, orchids caged

behind wire. The woman, pleasantly caged
in this conservatory, remembers her childhood passion:
how she spent her days with the flowers
in her father's greenhouse, trying to doctor
the pruned rejects he gave her; pale
cuttings that would not grow under his glass.

Now in this building, the moist glass
holds the breath of people and lilies caged
among *Passiflora Caerulea.* Its pale
green petals rise from a twisted stalk. Passion
Vine, its common name. She remembers the doctor,
throws a penny into the grotto edged by the delicate flowers.

In the cubicle, his standard speech flowers,
the words frighten her like cracked glass.
"If you were my wife, I'd cut it out," says the doctor.
The husband waits outside. The woman lies on the table caged
by memory of their brave passion.
She tries to speak brightly, but her words are pale.

"What about passion?" she asks, thinking it will pale
behind the mocking scars. His voice scatters like dried flowers.
"It's all in the mind, woman's passion."
She wants to disagree, but her throat feels like glass.

She tries to ask which muscles he will cut but is caged
in by the smile she is giving the doctor.

She can only imagine lying pale on a table behind glass-
windowed doors, the absence of flowers; caged
in a place beyond passion, her blood on the hands of the doctor.

This wild field,

this skeleton house: how the miner
brought his mail-order bride
here; how they insulated the walls
with German newspapers and once
or twice he brought her into town.
She was never seen again.

We could forget her forever
as her family must have tried–
waving her goodbye on the boat,
bending to their work every
morning, waiting for letters,
stalled in their arrival.

And perhaps we are all mail-
order brides, made to order
for exactly this life of moving
from place to place, engulfed
by mistakes, then never heard
from again. In this very meadow

must be her grave, the grasses
covering our loss. Is it here outside
the house? Or over there beneath
the knoll? I peel newspapers
from the wall, pretend I read
German, imagine her pouring

over and over this news
from home until
her husband rips the papers
from her hands, stuffs
them to the wall, and hammers down
the final layer of wood.

WOMEN'S RETREAT

–for S.S.

It's cold and wet.
Everyone is complaining.
No Bible verses or prayers.
One hundred women,
trying to imagine a world
without violence.

> During the break, we walk through mud
> and snow to the pond–its surface
> a black coin–below could be anything–
> albino plants, a rusted plow, the last
> gulps of a child struggling to the top.

> We talk of our mothers;
> yours, a recovered alcoholic trying
> to rewrite your childhood.
> Mine, unable to feed herself,
> having to call her husband
> to lift her from bed.

> Our own husbands, across the mountains,
> perhaps today digging gardens,
> our daughters spilling dirt
> and laughter everywhere.

Some say there are not enough prayers.
We think there are plenty;
could not bring Bibles or pretend.
We've already learned to circle
the pond; warned our children,
when swimming, not to drown.

CHRISTMAS NIGHT, TRAVELING IN A STORM

I used to imagine how it would be:
a dark night, but clear–stars
everywhere. Children asleep
in the back, their breath sweetening
the air, carols on the radio.
My husband drives, I rest my hand,
light, across his shoulder...

Silent Night is lost with the stars,
the children, too tired for sleep.
The night storm flies at our car,
endless specks of snow stab
the windshield. Dizzy, I search
for a line that will bring us home.

Always this: a snow storm hurled
from sky, ice teasing our wheels.
We follow whatever light we find,
freeze disbelief. Faith keeps
us traveling in the car
(our bodies braced). Faith,
and the slow wheels turning.

I I I.

I know now that woman
and painting and season are almost one
and all beyond saving by children.

–Linda Pastan

RETURNING TO RICHLAND

We cross the Columbia at Vantage
then start a slow climb up the cliffs;
I drive with my daughters beside me,
their father asleep in the back.
The children see only sky—
gray, streaked with red.
I do not tell them the river
lies black and sullen below.

The road levels and we travel
the miles from dusk to darkness
telling stories. I try to follow
the reckless plots, to ignore
the desert crusted with snow.

At the finish of every story,
we each get three M & M's,
our emergency ration packed
for crossing the mountains
in case we stalled in a blizzard.

The sky turns black long before
we reach Vernita, our headlights dissolve
in the dark. We keep retelling
the same stories, count our candies
like beads of a rosary

until we pass the Indian fishing ground,
their empty platforms the landmark
for all things that return.
I speed those last miles in silence,
mouthing my secret prayers,
and the desert, exposed now
in cold moonrise, recedes
as I drive us all home.

CAMERA OBSCURA, DARK CHAMBER

—for Dave

> The first crude camera was a huge box with a
> tiny opening ... to admit light. The box
> was large enough for a person to enter, and
> was used by artists... to trace the outline of
> the image formed inside.
> *—World Book Encyclopedia*

You could disappear for days,
on trips to Monterey or the wine
country, listening to poets
speak about silence.

And you could record
everything carefully, in secret
notebooks, or through
your camera's steady gaze.

And it would be alright,
watching cypress lean
away from absent winds,
remembering old movies

from Japan as you trudged
across the dunes.
But there is this other
thing. How drawing

your own life needs
to be shared. There is
this sound that whispers
these moments—sifting through

sand dunes, finding stray
shadows—*must be traced*
if only as a quiet
artist in a room of pain.
Then one day your father softly
admits he, too, has thought

about death. Or late
on another afternoon a woman

thanks you for being
a silhouette of her own father
or, perhaps, all the men
who ever lined the river.

Then maybe it is enough—
these slight snapshots we take
of ourselves, and others,
the ones we give away.

THE LOWER EAST SIDE GHETTO

Here is a picture of the East Side
ghetto, New York City, 1906.
My father is almost born,
though not here. Already
you can see his determined face
among men on this street.

And why do they pause to stare
at this panoramic camera as if
demanding a new history?
Some with hands placed defiantly
on their hips. Others, resting
their arms on the shoulders
of adolescent boys.

The photo is crowded with carts
and horses, crates of fruits
and rotting vegetables, all crushed
together in sepia tones.
Faded awnings hang
over shapeless women who yawn.

In this picture, I am sure,
is the old man who comes,
every day, to our desert river.
Italian, he's told me about
life in that kind of street.

Each day I watch as he pedals
his 3-wheeled bike to the water
exactly at noon, and tosses
day-old bread to hoards
of waiting gulls, as if
the crumbs were golden coins.

FAMILY INHERITANCE

We find you in the microfiche.
Andersen, Anders, born 1870.
Grandfather, there in blurred
white, your name static on the screen.
I want to trace my fingers
across the glass, but this
is no gravestone.

Sixteen, you leave your father's
home, come to the New World,
disinherited. No matter,
you're fluent in seven languages,
translate at the World's Fair
but end up selling pillows
door to door.

You marry Hannah, from Schleswig-Holstein;
she soon wears down from births,
her legs swabbed every night,
the bulging veins wrapped.
Of nine children, five die
from disease and a fall
from a runaway horse.

You crowd into a basement apartment
but, no matter, you're saving,
stuffing meager dollars into pillows,
promising Hannah, Sven, the others,
you will soon return
to the Old Country.

All winter, winds
blow off Lake Michigan.
In June, when you are almost
fifty, a last child is born,
Dorothy. You watch her grow
carrying these losses:
the pride of Danish aristocracy—
linens at the table every night;

the shame of Chicago poverty—
Hannah, on her knees doing laundry
in the tub; the pretense, always,
that things aren't as bad as they seem.

When you die of a vessel bursting
in your brain, Dorothy is only eighteen.
Two weeks later she returns
from the grocery where she clerks,
sees a note on the door to meet
at her aunt's and knows
Hannah, too is dead.
She circles the block
four times before allowing
the news to be delivered.

Here, in these files, your children
and wife. I can spin them forward,
silver threads on this black screen,
coming to the time
of your daughter's return.
How Dorothy journeyed
to the Haderslev churchyard,
stood by your father's grave,
asked him to forgive you
your reckless leaving, placed
her fingers on the stone,
finally, no guilt.

                    —for Mother, Dorothy Andersen Rogers, 1919–1985

MONDAY MORNING IN OCTOBER

You call, voice shaky;
because I was gone, we're three
days past our weekly talk.
*Oh Mother, I do not want
to forget.* Yet, it's difficult to wash
the breakfast dishes, peel each green
orange, watch gold leaves scutter
across the porch, or listen to the whipping
wind, without thinking of your pain—
each joint a pin of dissonance,
your weakness making white
pauses in our conversation.

My last visit, your body seemed
that hollow vessel I'd heard
about in Sunday School. At twelve
I could never imagine such a thing;
we were all flesh and blood and mine
was always beating towards some great
destiny. Now forty and still the same,
yet knowing what comes next is a slow
emptying, I sit at the window
where I've moved my desk to watch
the fall leaves.

My husband asks why I'm drawn
to this cold room, its large expanse
of glass. I do not tell him I want
to see the trees drop their separate
leaves, to watch each bush shiver
as it gives up its green, to listen
to the scatter of autumn debris
across the grass, to wager each day
on the prevailing wind.

THE POET BRINGS HER MOTHER
   TO HER READING

Your mother wears red
and black and so do you.
She sits under a black
umbrella of a hat and watches
you read. When you get
to the poem about the scourge
of dogfish, she smiles.

I envy you with her right
here. Not envy, but a trust.
I want to hug you both
for being together, like this.
A bitter woman will say,
*It's hard to write a positive
"mother" poem.* You will have read
the one where your mother
is beautiful.

I don't argue, but I want
to say that I, too, could write
a poem about my mother's beauty—
even in the hospital two months ago.
How the night of her final dying,
my brother and I sat with her,
sipped wine and shared the lights
of Phoenix beyond her balcony, propped
open the door so she could breathe
the warm air. She thanked us, gave
her dimpled smile, and with arthritic
fingers, practiced writing her name
on a Kleenex box.

The next morning as we gathered
her things, I found that last
Dorothy scribbled among yellow
cardboard tulips.
Now I sit in the audience
behind your mother as you read.

You are mouthing vowels so round
and full they overflow in waves
to your mother, and then on to me.

As a child, I'd skip stones
across the pond below our house,
try to count the rings.
Or, not old enough
to ride, I'd wander the fields
with the horses.

What I loved most were evenings
with them in the barn, the stomp
of their feet, the ticking
straw, closed air, and their
beautiful bodies, near.

I V.

For anything lacking–for trees, for rain,
for salvation–I am learning both sides
of the window, and standing between, turning to glass.

William Stafford

REMEMBERING YUCCA FLATS,
ONE FALL SUNDAY

As children we trembled from sleep
to sit on backyard fences
in the dark waiting
for a light too cold
to cast shadows. Trapped
inside the space from flash
to breaking roar, we counted
our fears in silence;
then watched for dawn
to bring the promise of warmth
and the cloud rising, majestic
in its mushroom form.

Since then, twenty-six years
have drifted away; we live
in a distant state. Knowing
the dust those clouds can rain,
I press my children's hands
like leaves I choose to save.

The white-robed minister
is eloquent this morning.
Lifting his arms like a lone
gull, he aims towards flight, speaks
of unknown power. The day
repeats his words in color,
leaves float through sky—a brilliant
scattering of quotations. At dusk
my family sighs, settles
around the fire. I know
my heart, consider the effects.

DEGREES OF LIGHT IN AN AFFLUENT CITY

Isn't this your life?
                    –Richard Hugo

You didn't come here on a whim.
Careful thought and a new job
and now you're smothered
with beauty–the browning
summer mountains, the always blue
sky charged, just as you get bored,
with electrical rain.

And the polished cars,
in designer colors. Money
wraps everyone in a ribbon
of labels and even old people
are tan, with strong biceps. Each
morning you wake to the soft
thud of runners pacing
down your street. Here,
everyone says *yes* to themselves,
imagines this is *their* dream
except for yourself who hears,
always, the endless traffic, the hum
and rush of BMW's churning
up the highways.

You know, now, why men drape
themselves with gold chains,
cannot collect enough credit
from the far hills to compensate
for beer cans and debris that float
the nearby creek. You find the homeless
who sleep in the library a welcome
relief from the profusion of white-
capped teeth, aerobic-tight
thighs, red hair dancing
on the downtown mall.

You long for the gray of your empty
home, the past life you traded

like some reckless poker hand
for this promise of ease.
And you knew, even then,
have always known, those derelict
towns, no matter how broke,
carry your real change. Even Hugo
remarked after reading there—
weak then, with only one lung—
your old town *wasn't so bad*.
And even before he said that,
you loved him, knew
that if he ever came to this light-
filled place, he'd understand.

CLOSING RANK

—for Fred Parr (1950-1993)

You could have stayed home,
storm so bad, schools closed.
Still, your husband's cousin's
death shocked, and you both
had this need to travel across
mountains, as if Fred's leaving
was an appointment
you had failed to keep.

      So, careful to wear dark
clothes in case you must go directly
to church, you drive—visibility thin,
ice thick—arrive with just enough time
to rummage the trunk for blazers;
enough time to almost forget
the accident you passed on Manastash Ridge—
body under bulging white sheet,
feet in hiking boots hanging out,
all that blood on the pavement.

At the Community Church police cars
arrive from everywhere, lights
flashing, sirens quiet.
Once inside, the policemen stand
in close formation circling the edges
of the room, over one hundred of them
in dress blue—so young, suddenly,
and handsome.

You didn't know this:
Fred, the nice guy you chatted
with at family gatherings,
who works in a lumber yard,
a reserve police officer
on weekends. It makes you want
to go back and start new
conversations, instead of
How's it going? Okay.

But today it's not okay.
He's dead at 43 of a heart attack.
A soloist sings, *I Will Always Love You,*
and everyone cries. Co-workers in gray
jackets stitched with Ponderosa Lumber
give testimonies and the minister
discusses Fred's life as metaphor.
It's not a half-bad talk considering
the preacher recruited for your mother's

service condemned you all to hell,
unless you'd been saved. But, we're here,
now, in Snohomish, watching Fred's family
leave as the officers step from the stage
offering each woman an arm.

So much unity and style!
You believe for a moment
they'll take care of us all.
And Fred's life in the outdoors–
tracking deer with bow and arrow,
then letting them go,
as everyone here must let him go,
the ending a wail of bagpipes
played by a lone man in kilts
who enters the church,
and walks slowly down the nave,
each note wavering.

THE SURGERY OF CHARITY

So it's the night before Christmas Eve
and the eleven o'clock news says the Mission
needs two thousand toys by morning.
Your teen-aged girls ransack
their rooms, for anything soft to hug.
But everyone wants more, so with checkbook
in hand you drive to the discount store.

It's one A.M., the store is filled
with people who smell of cigarettes
and bump into you while you fill
your cart with *Party Perfect Barbies,*
Totally Hair Kens, Ninja Turtles,
and five Santa Bears–marked down.
The next morning, early, you arrive
at the Mission, the line of people,
over a thousand, circling the block
and you're there with three sacks of toys.

This is also the day
your 83-year-old father's wife
will leave him. He does not give her enough
flowers and concern, she says, this bride
of three years, having just had open-heart
surgery. Sometimes, you'd like to perform
this ritual on all men's hearts:
open them up to their world–
small moments they might attend to.

But no, this is *your* generalization,
not all men close themselves
to the charity of feelings. Here,
at the Mission, a homeless man smiles,
right now, his face a veiny red. He holds
the door, saying, "Happy Thanksgiving."
And you enter, empty your bags, walk away.

REMEMBERING YOUR DEATH

–for D.R.

Here, we're far from town concerns:
traffic, mutated trees and the shade
they cast, how we darken our lives
with worry, the silence
we vow before we talk on and on
then wonder why everyone says they are lost.

It is no easy way out,
this rock-hard suffering,
this white-out of sound.
How the riddle of the fallen
tree in the forest means
nothing if we turn
only to ourselves, ease
into a trance.

       We pretend this bed
of today is what we lie in,
as if memory could erase
past events and we were able
to drowse in our intentions–
wishes without action, or the segmented
branches of your lungs breathing
loam fresh from deep woods,
not those distended sacs, heavy
with the fluid of pneumonia,
the water lapping inch by inch
to higher ground. Beauty
meaning only breath,
and air the last offering
we receive.

YEARS PAST THE HERON

There among rushes,
among the facets
of sun on green marsh grass,
among shadows, the river

curling around a wide bend—
there in the shallows, a heron—
long-billed, beautiful, standing
quiet, attentive as desire.

Summer vacation in Oregon.
Sun River. We paddled rubber Seveylor
rafts down the Deschutes past
otters, deer, and this one

heron placed for us, the family.
If memory would take that kind
of stance—hold up a regal
feathered head and place

both feet in the oncoming
water, then all the days
we regret, those moments
we beg forgiveness, would rush

by downstream. Or, if time's perfect
bones would gather like the wings
of the gray jays yesterday at camp,
(now we are years past the heron,

miles away, high in the Colorado
Rockies)—if remembering
would come only when
we were ready, then, perhaps,

we would know happiness. Oh,
if memory would cry for food—
a raisin, a cracker—then
suddenly appear and ease

the thick air as the wings
of the gray jays, thrumming
around our heads; if it could just
be like those birds

that kept flying in for landing
after landing to take only
what we chose to offer
from our open palms.

THE RAIN, HOW IT FALLS

–for Peggy Jensen Rogers (1919-1993)

The coffin, draped in yellow roses,
rolls down the aisle, past flowers
and balloons that hang
like stars in the sanctuary sky.

Earlier, her daughters covered
her face with white net.
I cried. They prayed;
closed the lid.

There she was–almost at rest
as the last week I was with her.
Midnight, time for the medicine;
I'd wake her, lift her head
from the pillow, place each pill
like a wafer on her tongue.

Sometimes you wonder how it all unravels.
A Mormon lady becomes your rowdy father's
second wife. She has family trailing
from her arms like streamers,
furnishes the condo with magnet
mottos and stuffed geese.
In those three years you came to care–
her books filled with quotes,
Have a happening day!
just like your mother's.

Now, we leave her on this rainy day
after the hearse speeds
through San Jose–a quick trip
to the cemetery with only
a brick wall veiling
the industrial street.

We stand around in the cold;
strain for conversation

with her real family,
the mahogany coffin balanced
on its metal liner, dirt
from her grave covered
with green carpeting, flowers
from the church leaning
against the mound
like exhausted children.

And they will bury her beside
her first husband, and returned
to his name; proclaimed in the service
she's with him and Jesus forever.

It doesn't matter.
Our last talk she said,
"I love you." I replied
nothing, pretending there
will always be time.

And now, too awkward to take
even one yellow rose from the coffin,
I turn away with my brother's wife,
who lights a cigarette as we walk to the car,
our spiked heels punching holes
in the wet earth.

THIS FINE STRAND

Mercy is intimacy with despair
  —Rev. Barry Cammer

One can live through acts of kindness:
wilted lilies arriving with tangled verses;
casseroles shuttled back and forth during
nights of snow; hands hauling up skein
after skein of empty nets hoping
to prove the fishermen are right—
there is abundance. The quick star
that burns the fabric of sky knows
all too well, acts of kindness
are like candles seen
through Christmas windows.

But mercy, mercy lasts longer.
Mercy drags you naked over winter
streets cobbled with February ice,
then wraps you in down. Mercy says,
I will slit each of your veins,
from top to bottom, watch
the blood drip, then sew you back up.
Mercy draws a picture of the world
and reveals nothing. Mercy
conjures up islands
of black tar boiling, leaves
you swimming to their shore,
then appears in this frail boat,
extends a hand.

INHERITING THE SACRAMENTS

There are moments captured
like multiple images in a fly's eyes—
segments of flute notes repeated
and wailing or maybe a series
of gold-leafed rosebuds painted
on elegant cups.

All this talk of objects
and their placement just avoids
the issue of bruises blooming full
on her thighs. She pretends
it never happens, that life
is a trade-off of minutes printed
on plastic keycards used in the door
locks of fancy hotels—slide
the good news in and you cancel
the old memories. How the presence
of a man's hands on a woman's shoulders
can be a gesture of great pain
or tenderness and sometimes,
we pretend violence when our own lives
are calm and bruises appear
like stigmata, blessing our bodies
over and over in a ritual
that is out of control.

ABSOLUTION

We beg forgiveness daily,
forgetting to lock windows,
leaving fortune cookies behind
in rest rooms, turning the knobs
on antique doors.

I come each week praying
for salvation. You are the priest,
confessor of my childhood,
pale rabbi. How nice if you
could raise your fingers
in a blessing, offer me this—
a new life.

But no, there is only the awkward
arrangement of cells—teeth
and tongue and heart, toenails
growing into delicate flesh,
vertebrae that declare independence
every morning, the faint beating
of fear that maps each breath.

I have desired and hated this cardboard
box since birth. I have craved
and damned this careful collection
of memories and now I carry
everything to you, lay it
on the frayed carpet
of hope—this is what I want:
make it all right.

A WORD BY WHICH A THING IS KNOWN

It is important, this naming–
how a woman who changes
her name at marriage
slips off her childhood

definition as she might a silk
camisole that shudders
with the slightest rustle
to the floor. How sometimes, long

after making love, she wakes
in the cool hours of morning,
and tries to retrieve that small memory
of silk, to feel its soft-tongued

words whispered across her body.
Still, she chose to shed that name
as I unraveled mine at marriage,
letting it trail back into the past

because of the future:
I saw children, small waifs,
tangled in hyphenated names;
or worse, wearing a different

name from mine–his name;
or my name only, and he their real
father, the one who conceived
them, perhaps in great passion,

perhaps indifference. And how
that other name for sex,
making love, is never really true
nor untrue, no matter with whom

or where. And how the wind
today is wild and fierce calling
out all the names of those children
who were never alive

in this world, yet were named.
Like my friend's daughter, Sharon, stillborn
at four months, buried now beside
the eucalyptus tree in her mother's backyard.

And how in spring the pungent
odor of those branches settles
in the warm California air,
giving the day a sweetness
that no one can name.

V.

There are many kinds of open
how a diamond comes into a knot of flame.

–Audre Lorde

You only have to let the soft animal of your body
love what it loves.

–Mary Oliver

MOVING ON

The fireplace displays
red brick. "Paint it white,"
the realtor tells the woman,
"for selling, we want continuity."

Just so, her days spin
themselves white as a whisper,
this smoke trailing down words
I will never take a lover,
the woman declares, her hands deep
in soap, her husband's arms around
her waist. She is doing the dishes
and he has surprised her from behind,
his large fingers grazing the bottom
of her breasts. Sometimes she likes
love that way.

It is a new month
and the drought is over,
agapanthuses fling long leaves into
lengthening days. One hundred
people will tramp through the house,
admiring her carefully pruned roses,
the new Berber carpet. The woman has placed
everything at right angles, the furniture,
her life, their future. Nothing escapes her;
she treads through the days like water.
Once she grabbed a life preserver,
but it yanked her out to sea.
Now she is slowly returning,
each hour a new beginning,
a new pill of bitterness
to forget she swallowed.

But it is written life, liberty
and the *pursuit* of happiness,
the psychiatrist tells her. She is puzzled
about him, about happiness.
The previous therapist, a woman
with bleached hair and a silver Porsche,

furnished her office in slate gray
and peach-colored leather, used words
like *pleasuring, journaling,* and told
the woman to ask for *Truth.*

This one has stains on the carpet,
coffee mugs buried among scholarly papers,
a reckless sense of humor. He uses words
like *vicissitudes* and *crèche.* He tells
the woman to ask for *Money.*

Nobody will tell her what is real.
How to go on living
among the linear injustice
we are born to, the pale throat
of vulnerability we long to slash.

The house sells; full price plus.
She is convinced it was the poetry
broadsides she hung in the bathroom—
over the toilet—all men,
they christened her home with hope.

The next week she goes to the chiropractor,
I am a vertebrate, she declares,
and I suffer. That night she takes
her husband in her mouth,
*this is how we'll define
the new world,* she says, *write
the words here, and I'll sing.*

"THE BRIDGE IN ITS WITNESSING"–Tess Gallagher

–after being given a new book of poems

That the water running over
Helen Keller's hands or the river
the widow crosses on the bridge
is the same family, water,
as the vapor in which I steam
rice; gives me the same passage
through life–that sometimes swollen
river that flows after intervals
of drought when we are caught
in what we claim is blindness
but is merely our inability
to comprehend the gentle
tapping of that first word,
water, and the messages
we keep receiving hand to hand.

COEUR D'ALENE, AFTER THE STORM

—for Ginny, as she finishes chemo

This heart lake is mystery;
spreads magic colors horizontal,
as if we were dumb mystics
who wanted only visions before our lashes,
no left-brain prescriptions to blister
our senses or make us forget mother
earth–this cycle of water-becoming-cloud–
and the prayers we must say in our sleep,
offering each day as a blessing in a rhythmic
dance, like magicians who twirl scarves
over water, turn it into wine
as fast as this pale blue tint
washes gray sky after rain.

GOOD-BYE, GOOD-BYE

That old guy, there, he's afraid of death;
but you, you're afraid of life!
                    –Harvey Pirofsky

Perhaps to you it's simple,
this breathing from day to day,
only small gasps appear
to remind us we are inhaled
by our past, formed by fear
of our future.

You've heard it all before,
this low-pitched whine
like the hum of trucks traveling
too fast down Middlefield,
that tree-lined street that
borders your office building; a square
of concrete with courtyard and doors
that open and close every hour–
the people coming out, going in;
wooden figures in a cuckoo clock.

And we're all related, those
of us crazed enough with pain to pay
the clock–fifty minutes,
fifty minutes.

This hour, turning into memory–
a few notes jotted in your file.
Years from now, perhaps, you'll be reading
some book, some fine book in Palo Alto,
and think, vaguely, *What*
was it now? Who?

No matter; I'll remember your passion
for the written word: dusty papers,
books titled *Clinical Psychiatry*
(Haven't you read enough of that by now?)

last summer's *New Yorker's* abandoned
in the waiting room. I have gathered in
your walk—the tragedies
of others carved in your back—
how you end the hour,
both hands on your knees,
slapping them gently, *Ahhh, well...*
As if there had been
just enough time to listen.

SURVIVING A MOVE

Dear Anne, You're leaving again,
this time from a sky so flat and gray
you have to peel it back to find the sun.
Still, when you pack that last bauble,
say a macaroni star your first-born made,
or a white china mug etched with blue
trees, try not to think about the dogwood,
the meadowlark. There will be time
later, at the Shore, resting lizard-like
in the sun. Time to remember our desert
river, so unsettling on windy days
you longed to travel to the island,
hide among winter geese.

Gone, you can remember our meetings—
how we created in spite of cigarettes,
children, men. How the space
between words made lives easier.

You will have these separations:
the River, the bookstore, your friends.
But we will come, later, bringing books—
Forché, Waters, Sexton. You will shake
out your white lace tablecloth, folded for years,
and little desert spiders will scurry for cover.
(You've learned what they eat,
how they survive.) We will sit,
pass out poems. The sun will shine
through wood-framed windows, warm
the stucco walls. And we'll read
this poem together, say,
"It 's right, it's done."

LAST POSTCARD FROM PORT TOWNSEND

It's the same breath
that carries us, the same
perpetual cry of gulls.
How this riff of waves

against the shore exists
also in our inner ear.
The salt water that runs
through us, is around us.

The dome of sky that opens
this morning in Port Townsend,
this glass-blue sky that breaks
everyone's heart, is the same

as my own heart now opening.
And if, as a writer I am
to copy down this place;
or if, as an artist, I am

to sketch you one final
mirror. Or if, as a reader,
I am to understand any existing
line—where it came from,

where it is going—
the ferryboat that glides
across the Strait tells it all:
this day is a vessel for travel.

HITTING THE HIGH SPOTS

–for Jeanne

So I'm back in Palo Alto
on a *recherché* of sorts
and we're out for a night on the town,
which means hitting two bookstores
seven miles apart.

                    The southern store
has bright lights, gritty floor, girlie mags,
and, outside, a resident homeless in a watch cap
who washes our windshield
for, first, seventy-five cents,
but soon we're having so much fun—
the slight wire of fear–
he's washing all our windows
and we're in a corner of the dark lot
our doors unlocked. Jeanne tells him,
"I'm sorry, I have no more money."
He looks her in the eye and says,
"Never be sorry, honey, never."

And though we know he's a wino,
suddenly, we don't care
and I'm pulling dollars from my wallet
like rabbits from a hat
and handing them to Jeanne
who says, "My friend found some money!
Oh, and here's her bridge fare!
Whoops, here's another dollar!"
And the man, black and skinny
with pumpkin teeth, is scrubbing the windows,
repeating in a high-pitched whine,
"Thank-you, Thank-you, now don't you be sorry,
ladies. I had a job and I lost it
and I lost my place to live,
and I don't got no money."
And now he's polishing the mirrors
and we're wondering if we'll ever

get away and he says as we hand him
the final dollar, "God Bless you ladies,
God Bless," then wanders into the night
and we haven't even begun the evening

          which includes a drive north
to the upscale bookstore where everyone's
dressed in natural fibers and hundreds
of calendars drape over hangers
like tablecloths in a dry cleaner's—
a feast of days. Twenty-three years,
three states, and two kids earlier,
I met my husband here. But this

is Silicon Valley, now, and though the place
is swelling with all kinds of books,
aisle after aisle of art and literature,
everyone's crammed into a small space
marked Computers.
Jeanne and I laugh, thumb through the lit mags
till we find one of her poems,
open it up and spread it on top
of the macrobiotic cookbooks—food for thought—
hoping someone will stop and say,
Look, a poem!

But it's no go so we cross the plaza
to Cafe Verona where everyone
is either under thirty or over sixty.
Where are the others, we wonder,
working two jobs to live here?
Still, we stand in line for latté
long enough to check things out
and see who looks at us (the old men
whose wives are with them)!
And we listen to the Dixieland band
playing those intricate notes—
it's all in the rhythm,
the upbeat momentum they create
following us back into the night
where we drive home
with evening lights
shining through clean windows.

RELATIVITY

The woman never imagined
she'd spend twenty years with him.
Still, her life was charged
with the physicist, their discoveries
moments of exponential happiness—
like the time she was pregnant
and he placed his hand on the first
kicking, or the afternoon
they made love on Blue Mountain,
breeze chilling their skin
in spite of laser sun. And surely,

this is the reason it's lasted: his powers
of concentration exceptional, his attention
to the details of her body—each precise
crevice and fold; the anti-gravity
of nipples rising; and the momentum
of her ecstasy—these fascinate
the physicist in ways the woman
remembers for days. And so the equation
between them gathers its own velocity,
the force of their magnetic fields
an energy even he can't measure.

FOR BILL

I. *This Water*

The sea has darker lines
tonight. Fish forget
how to swim. Boats are slow
to consider their own return.

Years are not like fish staring,
nor grains of sand. Certainly
we can count our memories
as years, the years as agates, buried.

Each wave reveals what
we already know. Every drop
of water gives up its light only
when asked. This light becomes
the way we know the water.

Darling, we are bathed in light.
All changes matter.

II. *These Wildflowers*

Your hand. The shudder of dawn.
Believing in all choices of fire,
the limits of night, I am
with you, myself, a mirror
that no longer shatters.

And more.
The years become our own
mirror. The children's voices.
Their fingers, delicate
as lupine. Our trips
across the mountains
in bad weather.
How our talk
steadies us.

STILL LIFE IN THE PHYSICAL WORLD

We desire this ripening—
green pears in southern windows,
shiitake mushrooms nested in a basket
from the corner grocery—
all the abundance of duty
and want.

No, what I want is more.
How our lives collide
like strange sketches,
your small talk no different
than a woman's. You are
my double, the mirror
message I leave for
the visitor who pauses
in the hallway.

The mind creates the world,
but the body inhabits it,
draws all the edges we count,
such as index finger
tracing background air.

Or, say we walk beside the river
on this brilliant day. How different
to have hair defined by tree,
clothes outlined by water.

Still, there is always the body
displayed against sheets—pale
green or deep lavender. And
there is this, the *best*
any artist could ever do:
the body outlined by body—
arm across thigh, head
to belly; this is the portrait
we most desire, each of us
separate, revealed
by the other.

AS WHEN A FLY LANDS ON YOUR PAGE
AND YOU CAN READ THE WORDS *IT IS*
THROUGH THE WINGS

and you are camping at White River
having yesterday hiked past ten
waterfalls up to the Glacier, rested
in translucent sunlight beside

the milky stream while
your daughters gathered stones
searching for copper–
residues of the old mine.

And last night you lay
in your tent, the family together
in sleep, and you listened
to all their wandering breaths–

And this morning you're aware
of the constant tumble
of rocks, a low hum within
the fluent river.

And your husband serves
coffee while you are reading
in this moment of sunlight paused
between hours of trees.

And you know that beauty
lands sometimes, but never
by chance. *It is*
this fly, this page, these wings.

NOTES

- And the white-haired jeweler from Denmark is carving
  A perfectly faceted wife to wait
  On him hand and foot, quiet as a diamond.

Sylvia Plath, "On Deck," *Crossing the Water*, Harper and Row: 1971.

- "The Wren In Price Chopper" is after a poem by Pattiann Rogers, "For the Wren Trapped in a Cathedral," from *Splitting and Binding*, Wesleyan University Press: 1989.

- ...salt margins
  and stones that pulse...

Margaret Gibson, "In the Desert," *Out in the Open*, Louisiana State University Press: 1989.

- "The Woman Who Walked Into The Sea" is after a poem by Dixie Partridge, "For The Man Who Walked Into The Sea And The Woman Who Saw Him."

- I know now that woman
  and painting and season are almost one
  and all beyond saving by children.

Linda Pastan, "Ethics," *Waiting for My Life: Poems by Linda Pastan*, W. W. Norton: 1981.

- For anything lacking–for trees, for rain,
  for salvation–I am learning both sides
  of the window, and standing between, turning to glass.

William Stafford, "Tracks in the Sand," *My Name is William Tell*, Confluence Press: 1992.

- "Degrees of Light" is after a poem by Richard Hugo, "Degrees of Gray in Philipsburg" from *Selected Poems*, W. W. Norton Co.: 1973.

- There are many kinds of open
  how a diamond comes into a knot of flame.

Audre Lorde, "Coal," *Coal;* also *The Norton Anthology of Literature by Women*, W. W. Norton Co.: 1985.

- You only have to let the soft animal of your body
  love what it loves.

Mary Oliver, "Wild Geese," *Dream Work;* also *New and Selected Poems*, Beacon Press: 1992.

- "the bridge in its witnessing..." is from a line in Tess Gallagher's poem, "Moon Crossing Bridge" from *Moon Crossing Bridge*, Graywolf Press: 1992.

ABOUT THE AUTHOR

Gayle Kaune was born in Chicago and spent her childhood in Michigan, Florida, Alaska, Nevada and California. She holds a B.A. from Occidental College, M.A. from Stanford University and an M.S.W. from Walla Walla College. Her poems are published in literary magazines and have won four Washington Poets' Association awards and a Ben Hur Lampman award. Her chapbook, CONCENTRIC CIRCLES, won the Flume Press Award, 1989.

Kaune has worked as a teacher, adoption caseworker, and psychotherapist and lives in the Eastern Washington desert with her husband, William Kaune. They have two daughters.

ABOUT THE ARTIST

Ann Bowker lives in Yakima. In addition to painting and teaching, she is a jeweler and designer of wearable art. She exhibits widely, and is known for her paintings of Egypt, African animals, and Yakama tribal figures. Her painting for *Still Life In The Physical World* is her first book cover.